Sharon Louise Barnes
Artist Statement

"there's a deeply soulful aspect about making meaning out of things that have been rough"

Although I will always be a painter, in recent years I have become absorbed with working in interdisciplinary processes using rough, salvaged, and industrial materials. There's a deeply soulful aspect about making meaning out of things that have been rough.

I am inspired by the idea that the reality of our rough issues and rough circumstances can be altered and even transformed if you exercise enough sustained will to struggle through the challenges that are presented by them. By choosing the frequently rigorous processes of working with rough and disparate materials, my art is informed by metaphors about struggle, hope and transformation, while I frequently visit themes of social justice and the complex politics surrounding race and women.

All images ©2017
Sharon Louise Barnes

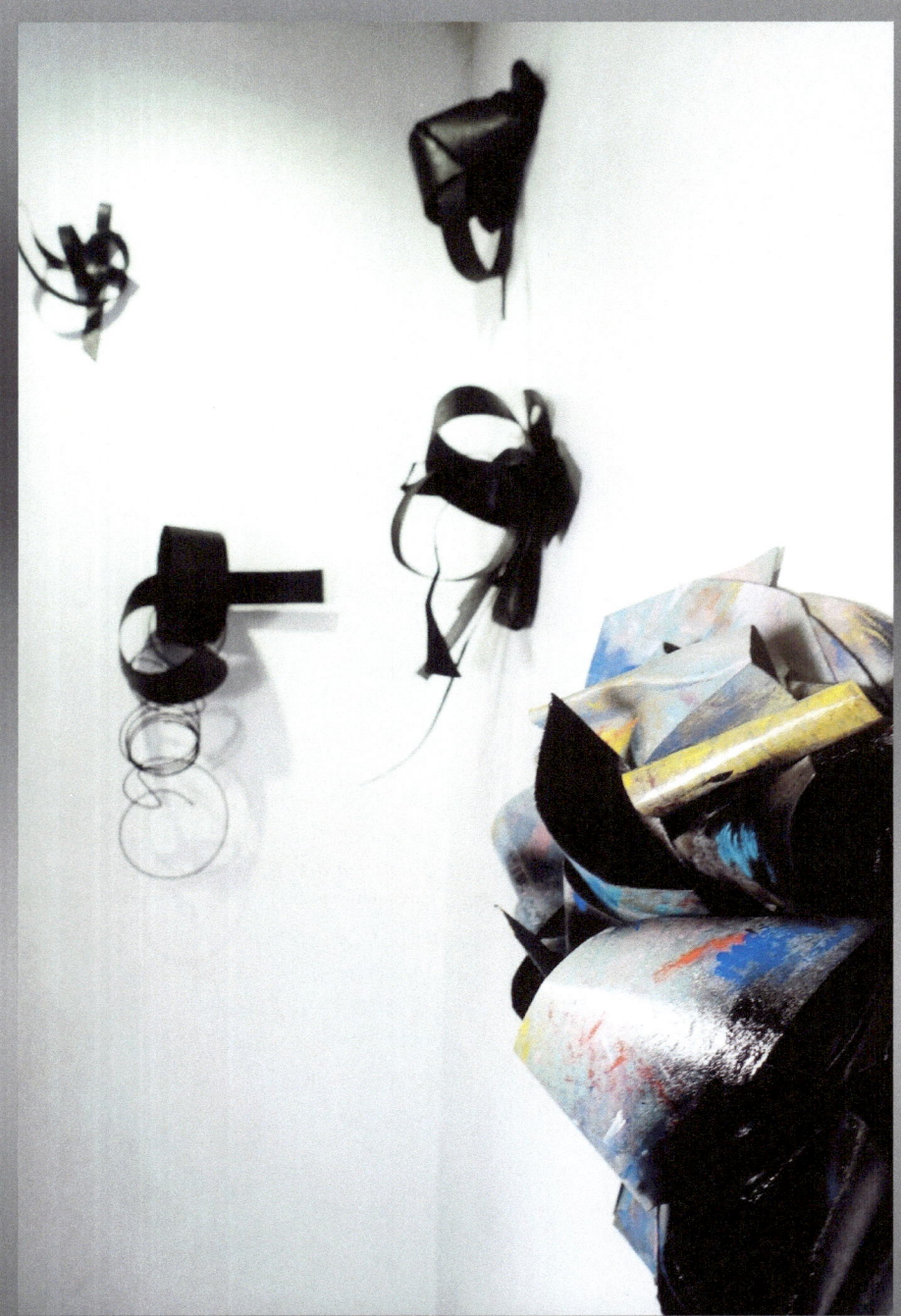

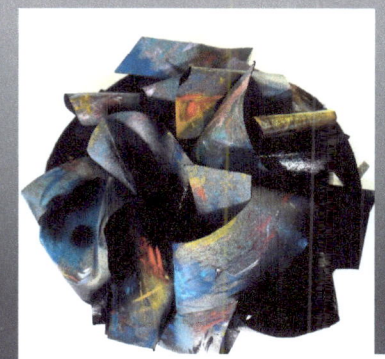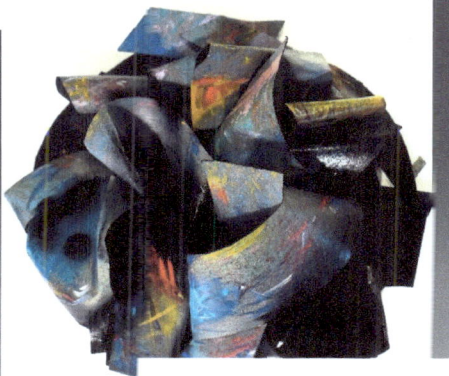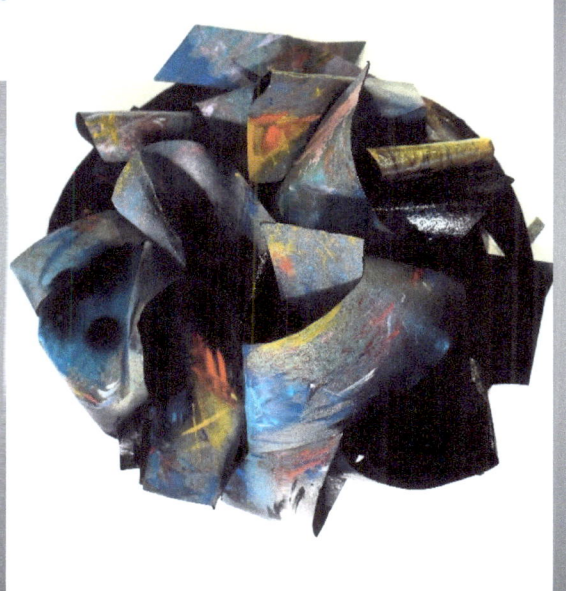

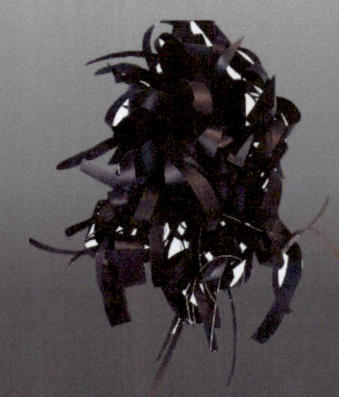
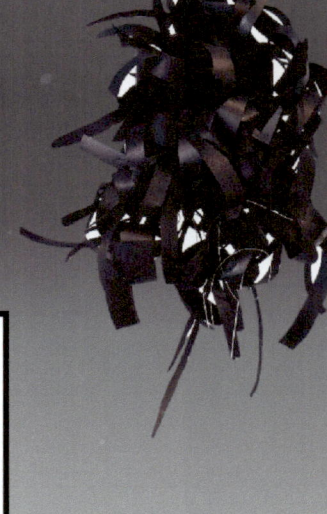
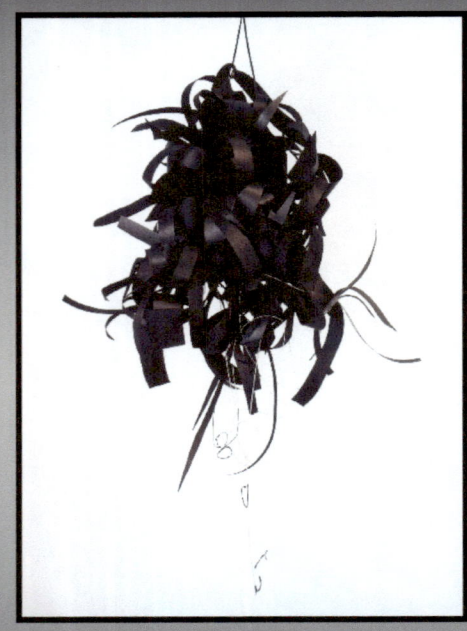

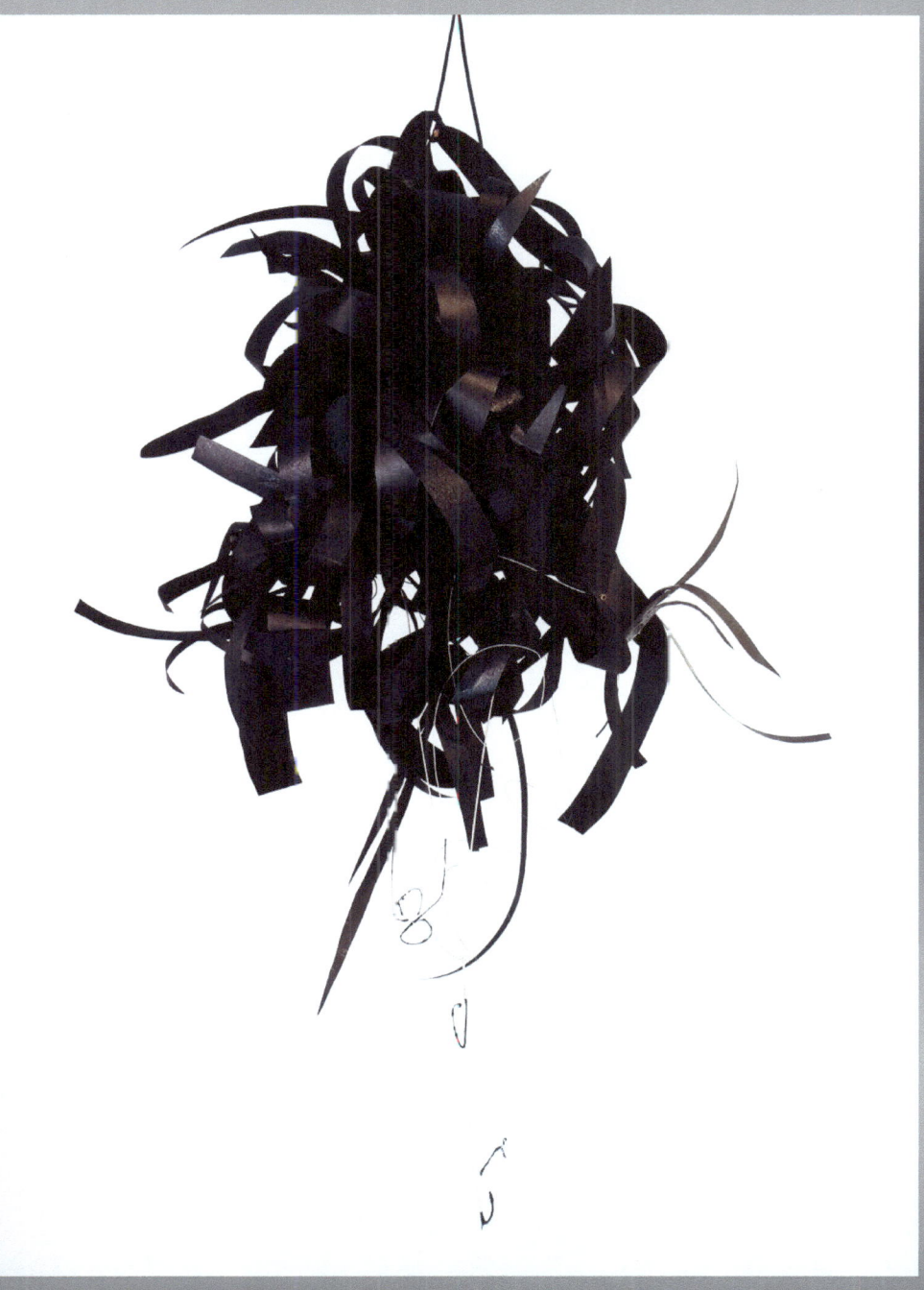

"humming in the night" (2017)
industrial roofing paper, black lacquer, guitar strings, wire

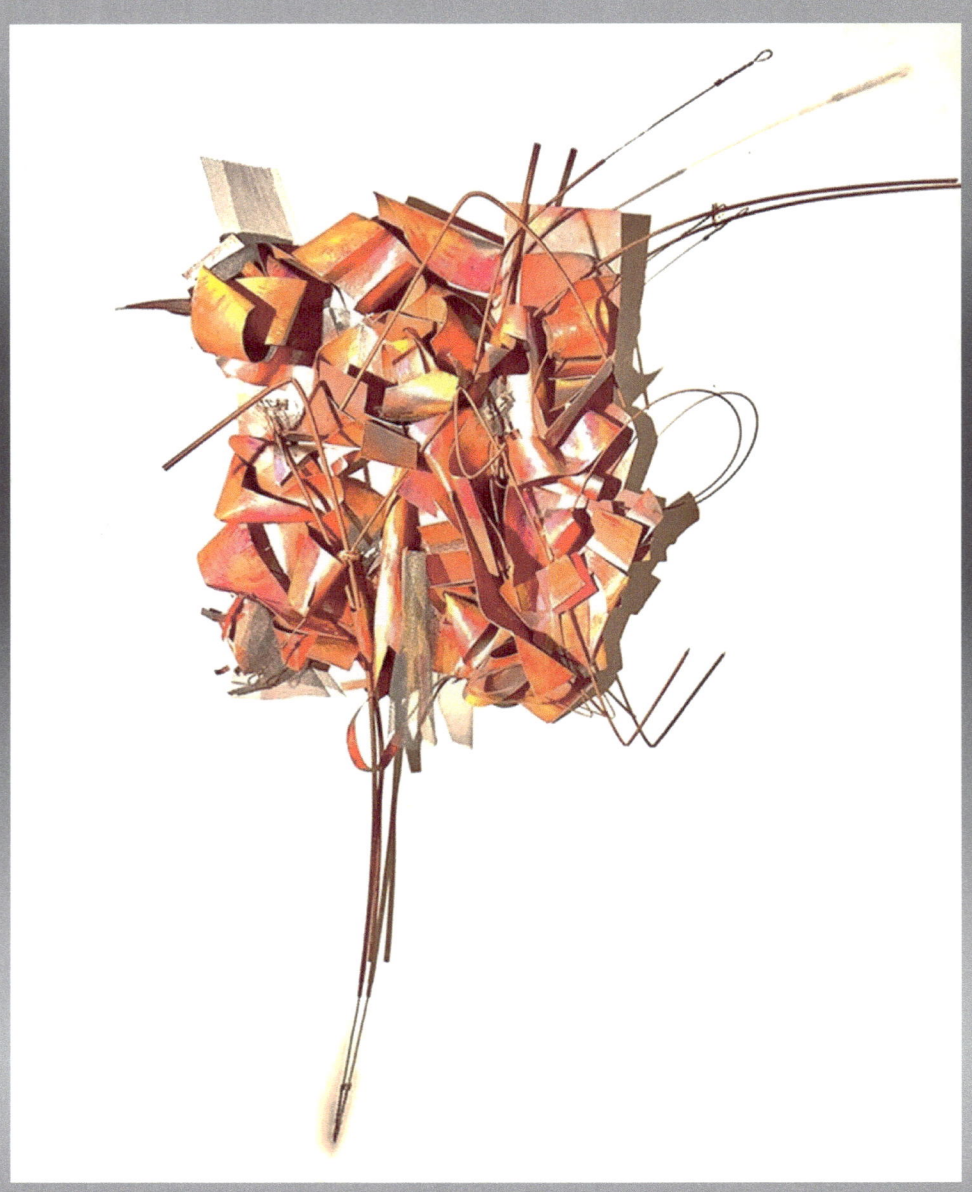

"humming in the night no. 2" (2017)
industrial roofing paper, vintage piano strings, acrylic, resin

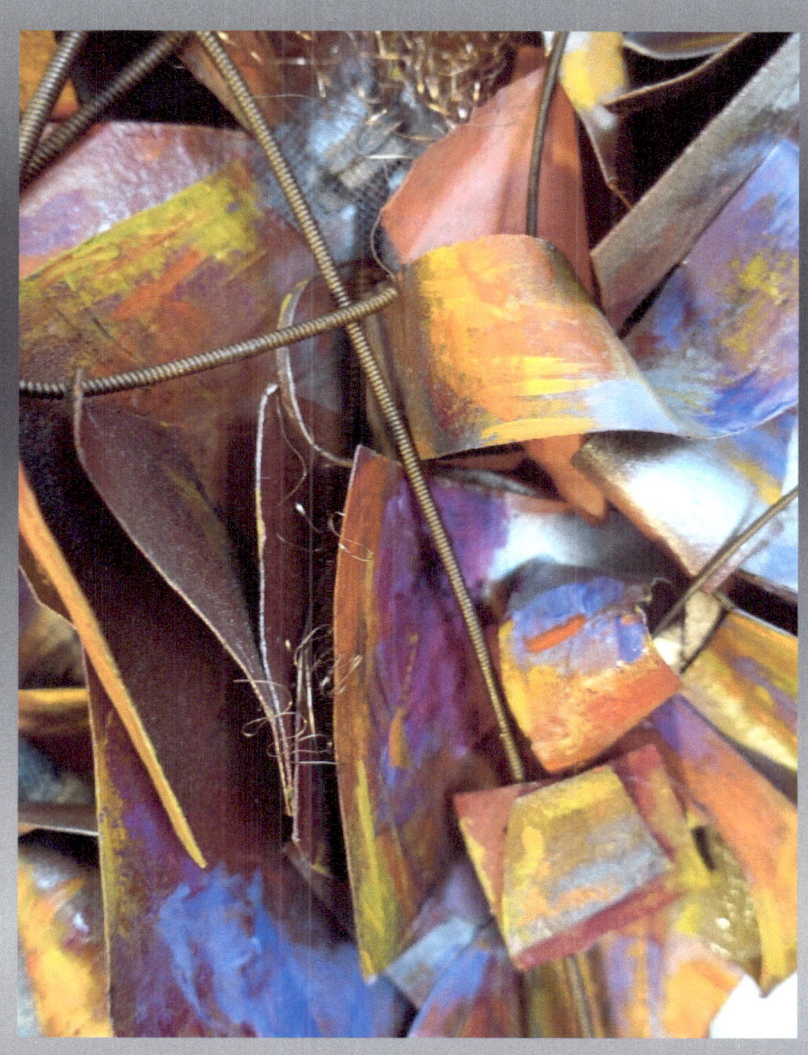

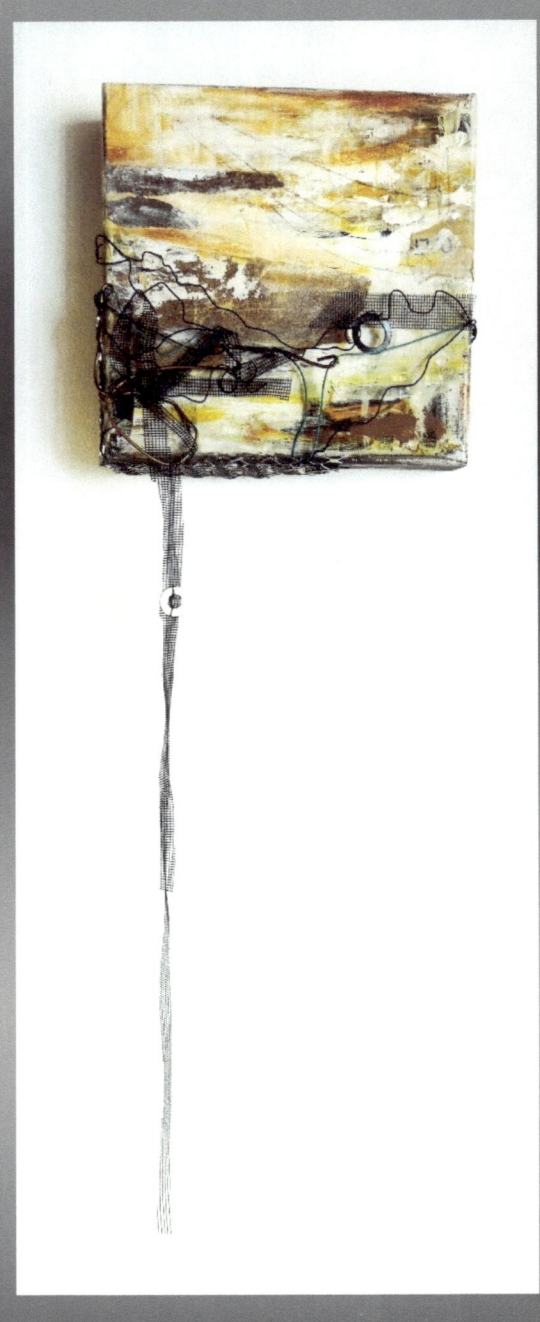

"Beauty like fine grade sandpaper"
acrylic, sandpaper, wire, screen, on canvas

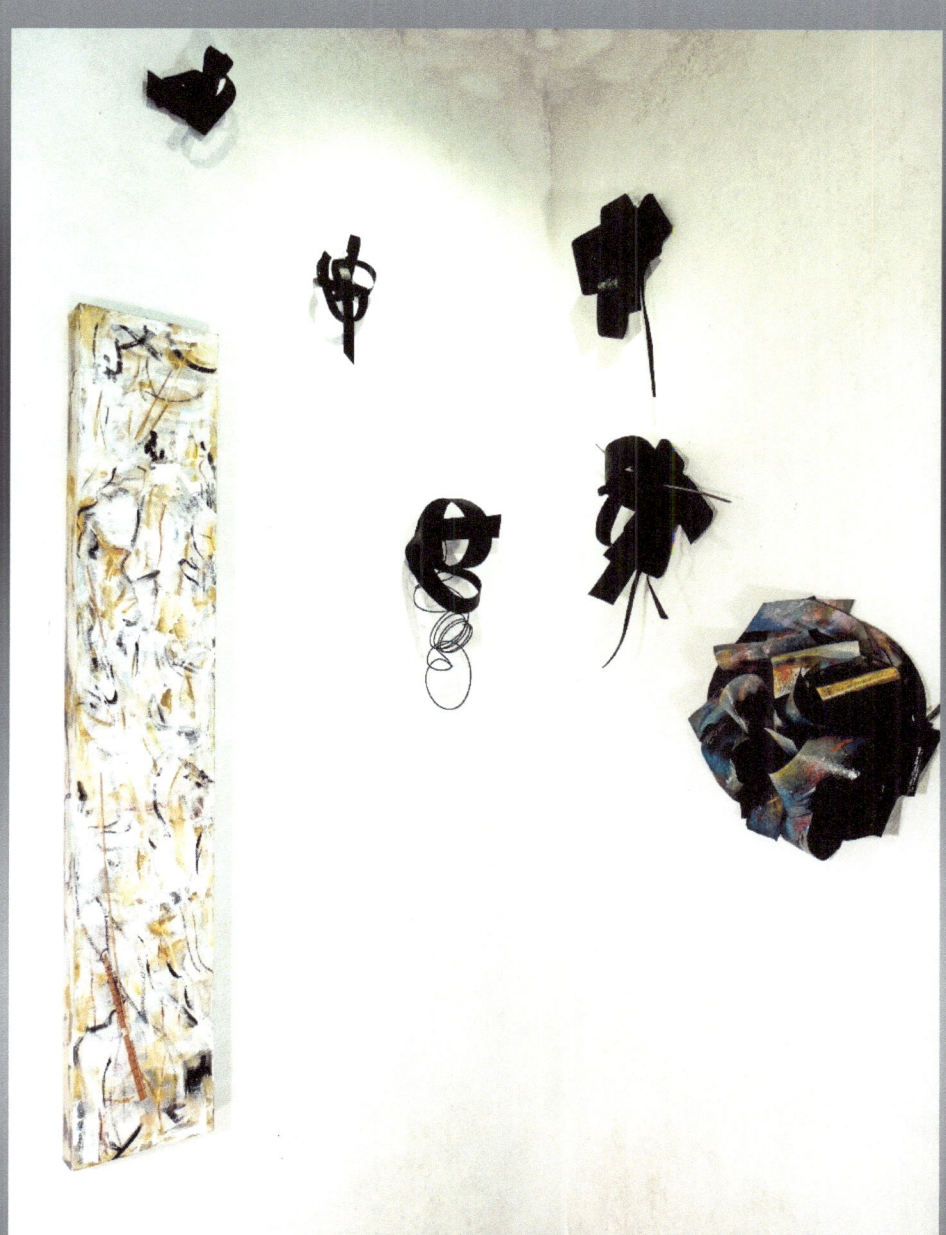

My series of sculptural works and hybrid paintings using prepared industrial tar paper, hearkens back to the racially loaded and disparaging term, "tar baby" -- but then re-claims and transforms the term, flipping it on its head.

My "tar baby" works become the rebuttal to the disparagement, instead messaging beauty, poetry and providing a platform for social commentary.

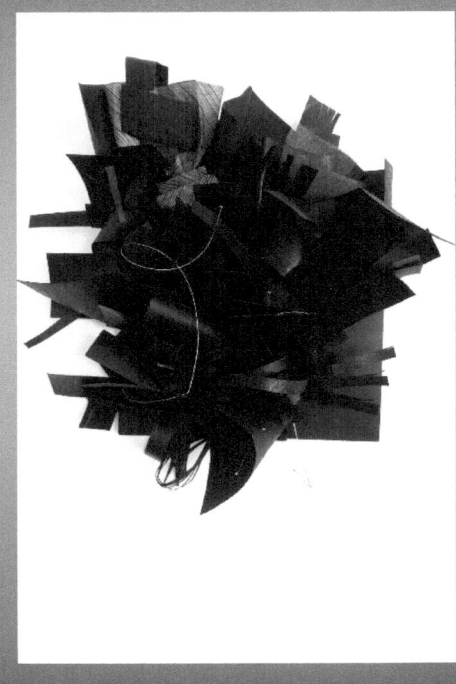

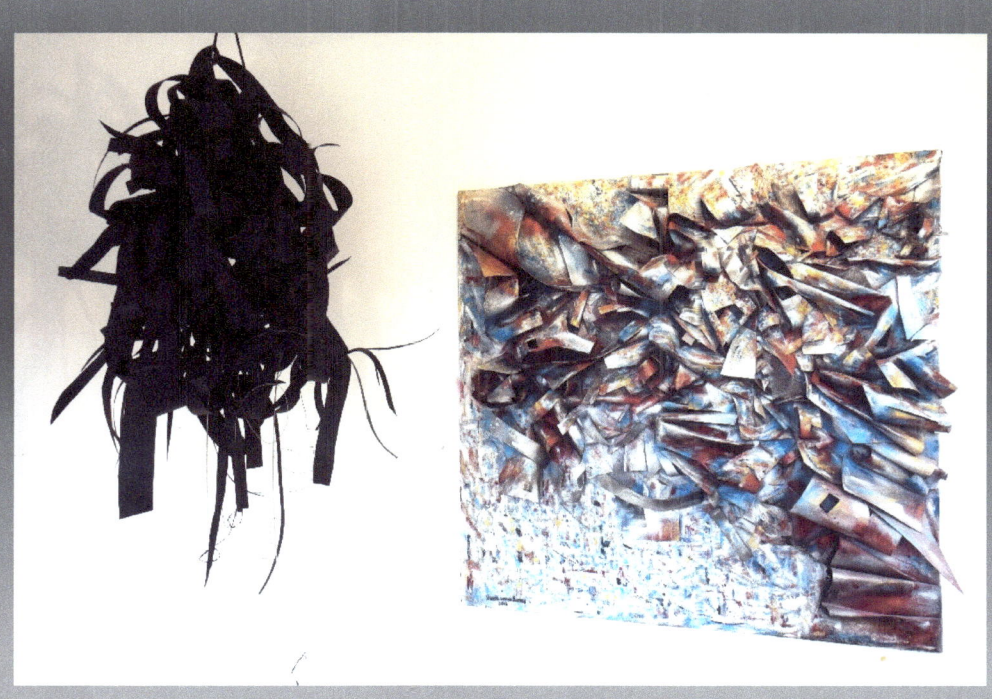

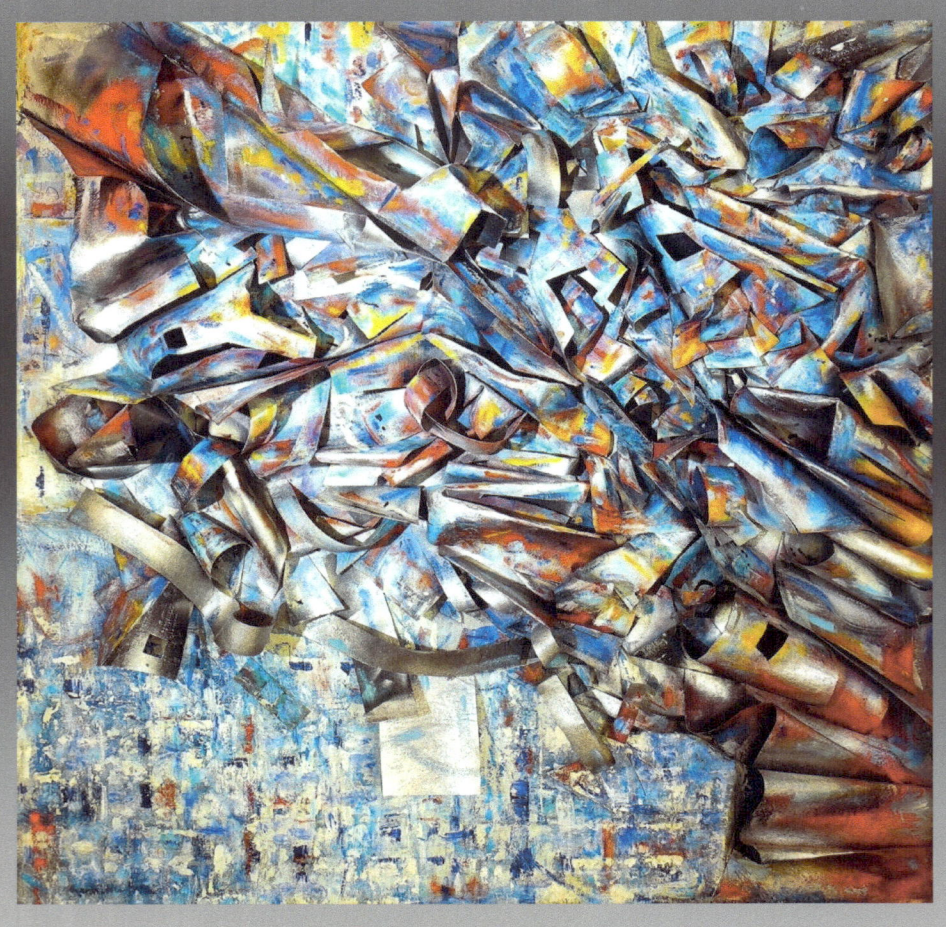

"the debris in our collective stream of consciousness "
(2016)
48" x 48"
industrial paper, acrylic, oil, spray paint, wire

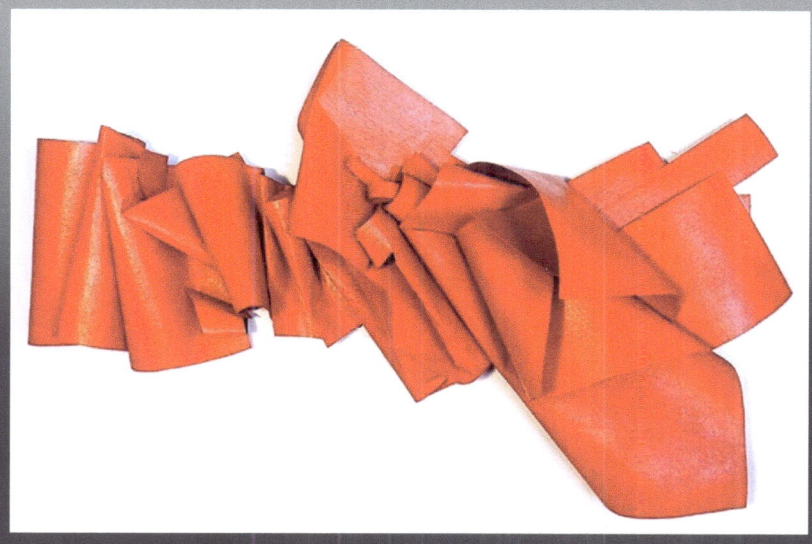

"Détente, the negotiated easing of a hot situation"
(2016)
Industrial paper, acrylic on bamboo
26"x39"

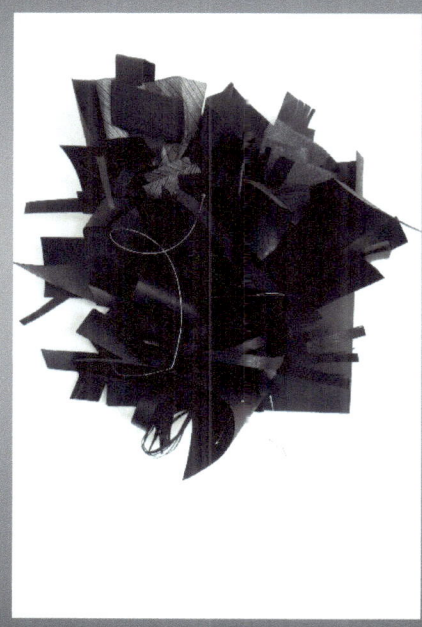

"all black everything"
(2017)
industrial paper, violin strings, Japanese paper, lacquer
22"x18

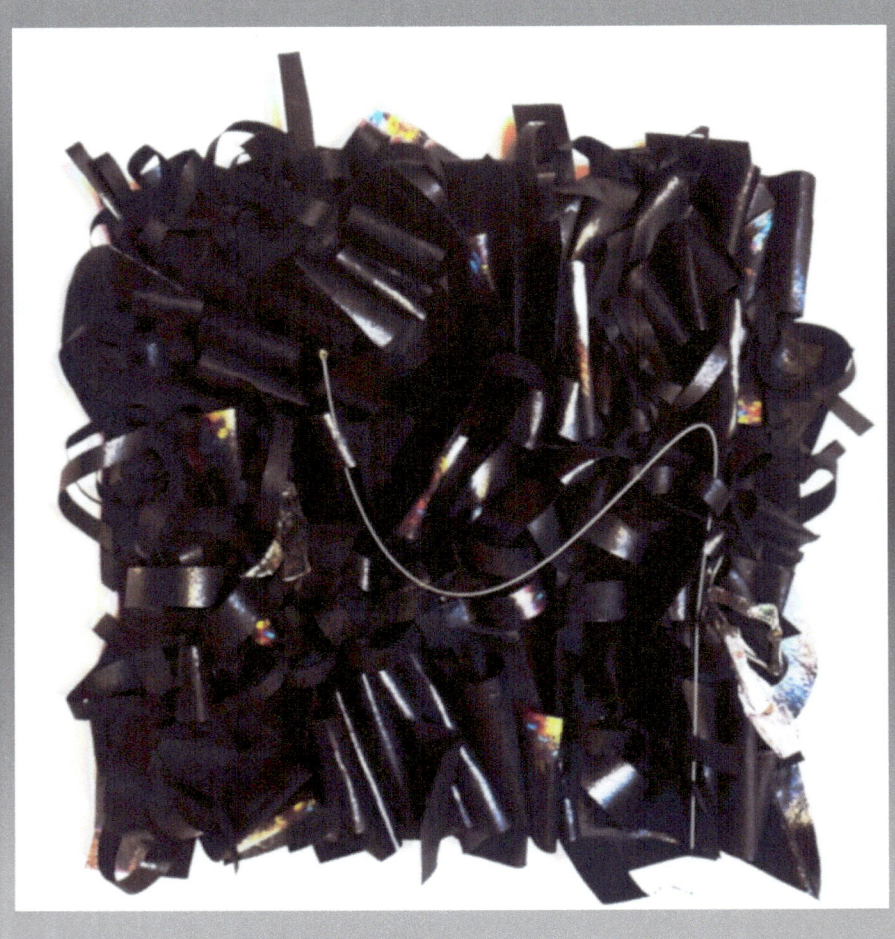

"the nuances of color"
(2017)
Industrial paper, guitar strings, lacquer
24"x24"

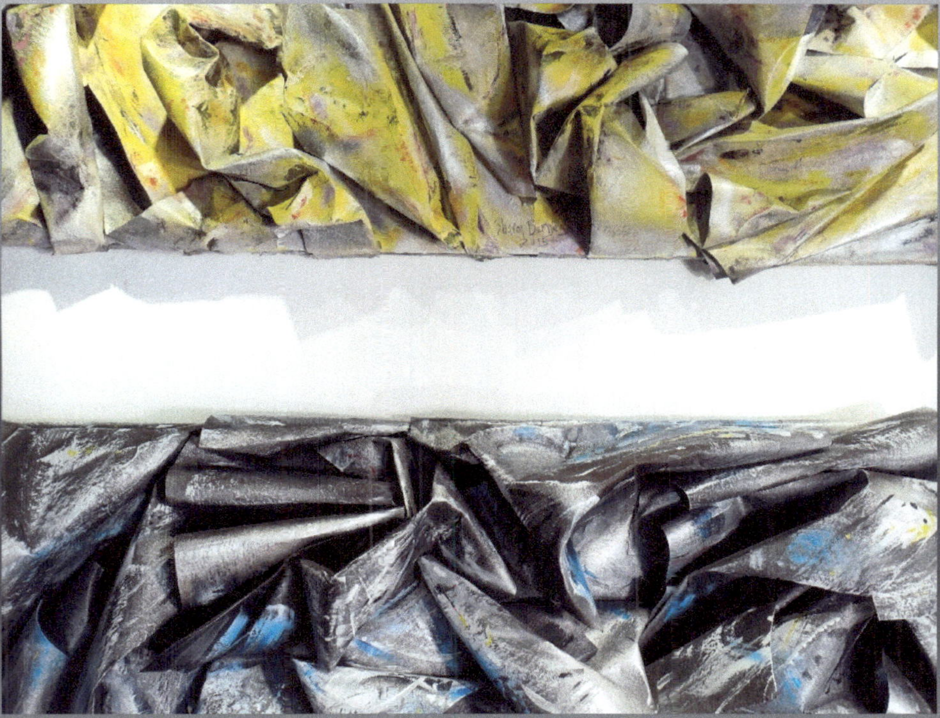

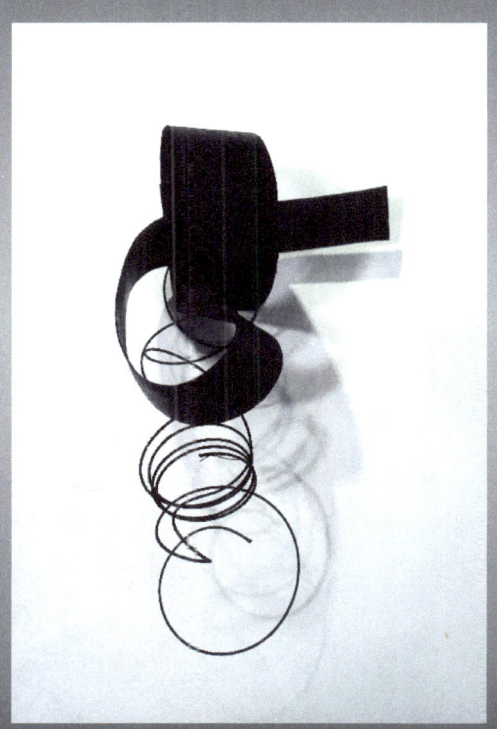

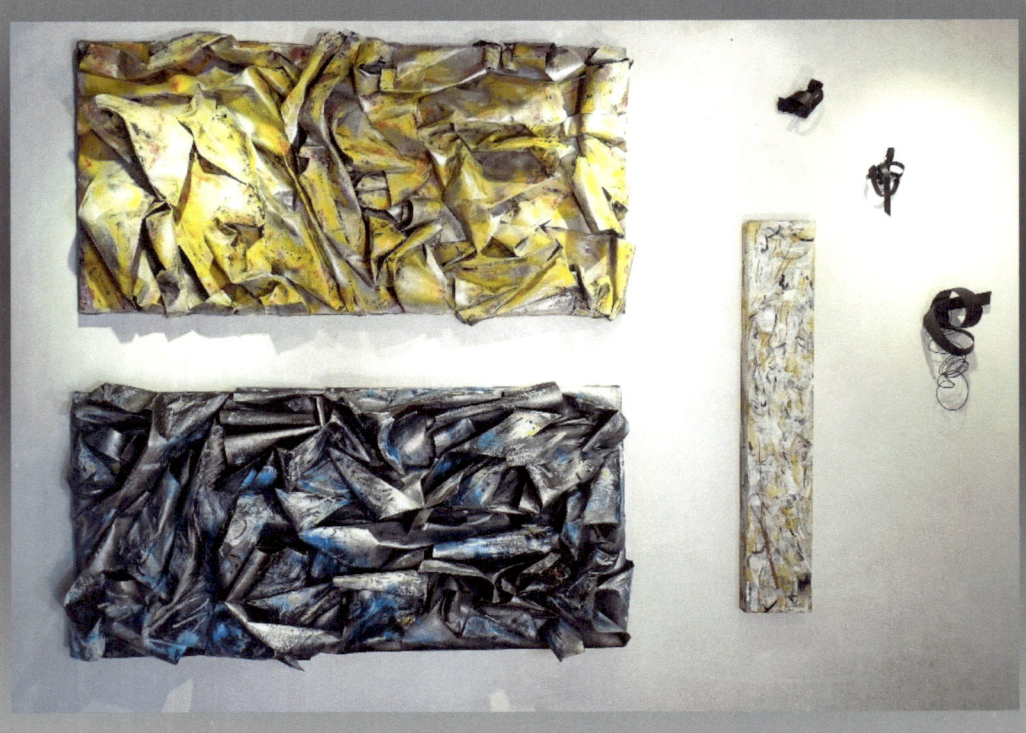

(Left) Playing Fields: Not Flat, Not Level (diptych)
(2017)
mixed media relief sculptures 24"x48

"Trickle Down"
acrylic and mixed media painting on canvas (right)

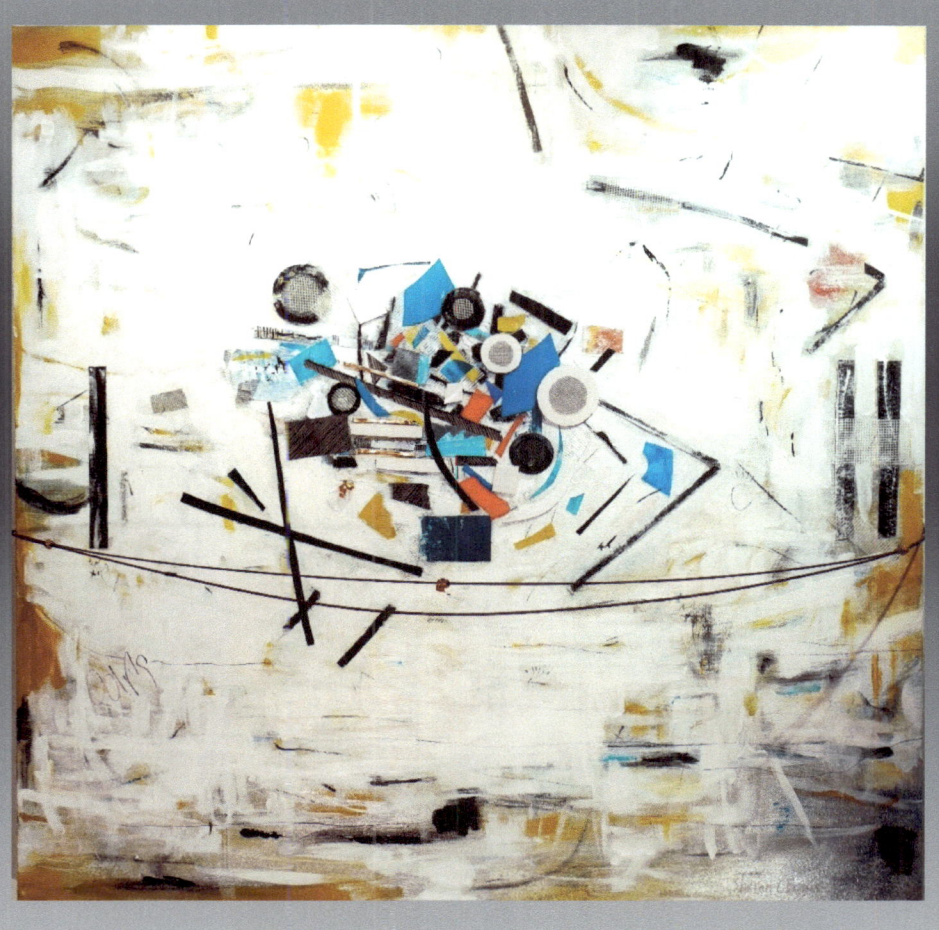

Bang (2017)
Acrylic, paper collage, copper, piano strings on canvas
36" × 36"

"moon kissed and touched by sun, her magic is unwritten"
 (title after the writings of Audre Lorde)

acrylic, enamel, photo transfer on gauze, salvaged fiber
on canvas
(2017)
18"x18"

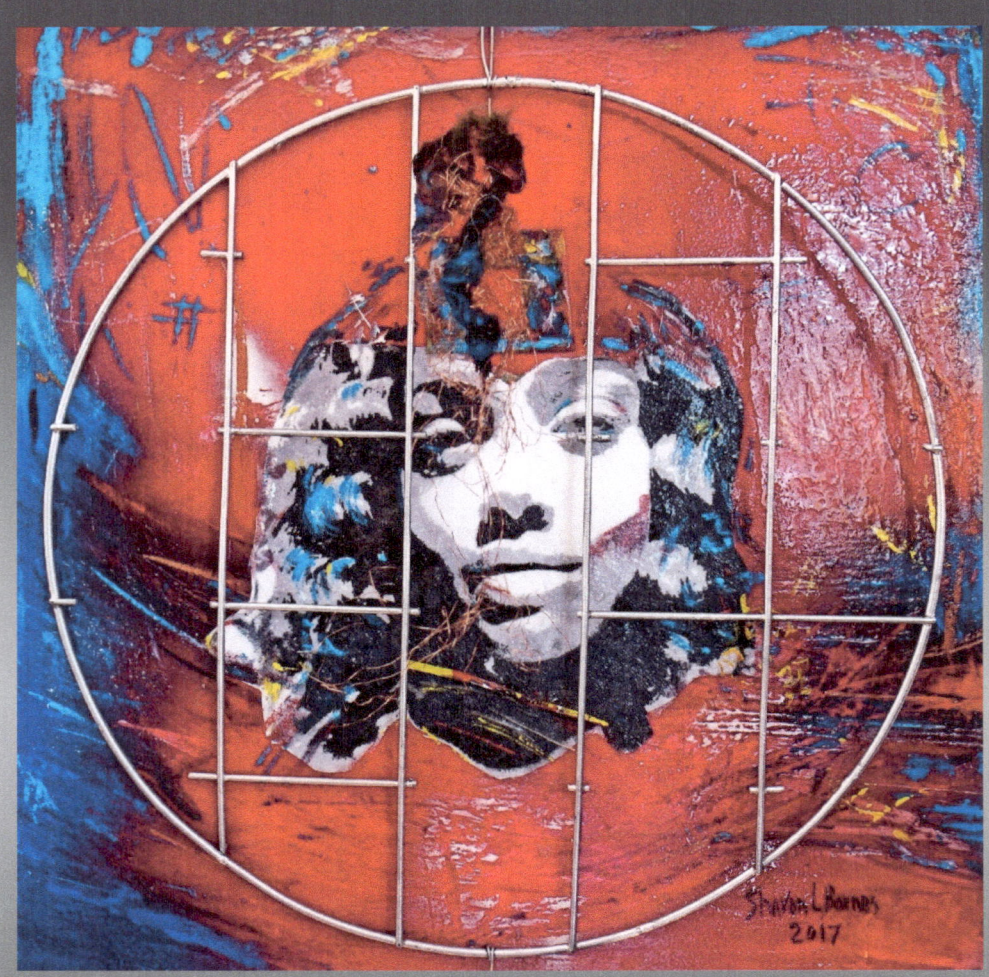

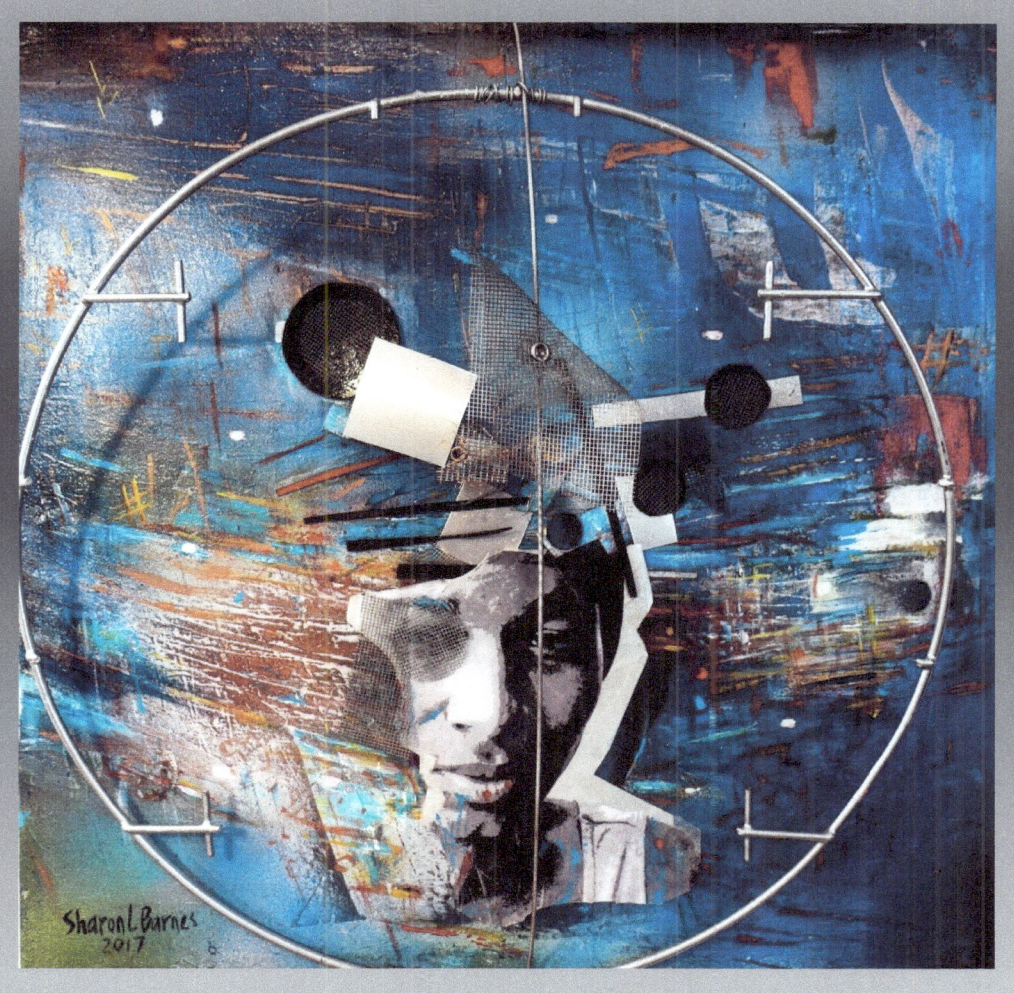

"just because we're magic"
(for Jesse Williams)
(2017)
acrylic, enamel, industrial paper collage, photo transfer, metal,
salvaged objects on canvas
18"x18"

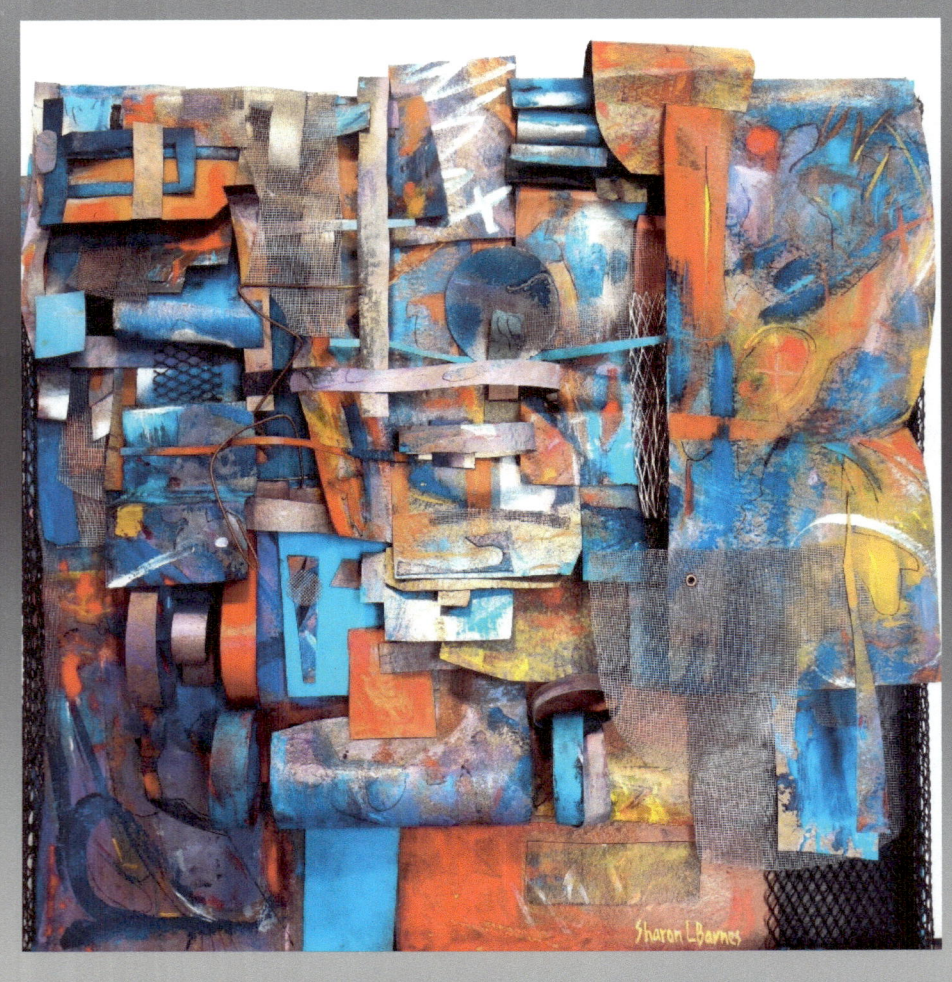

"Whaat" (2017)
mixed media paper collage, wire
24"x24"

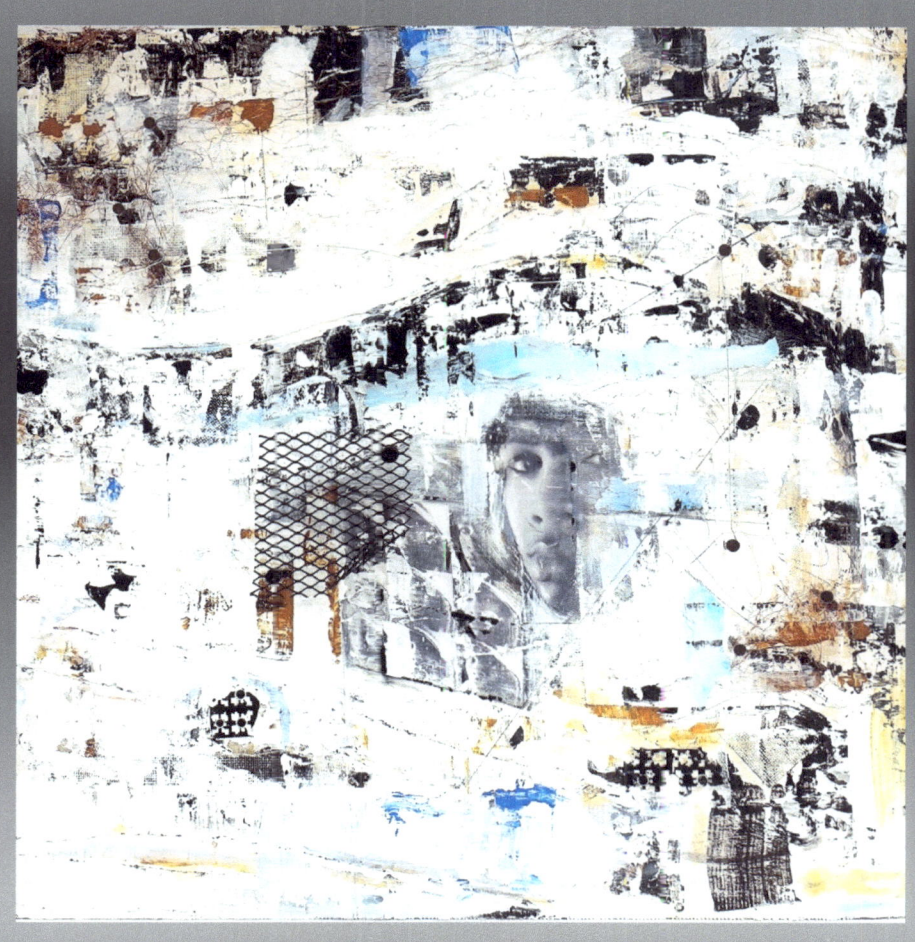

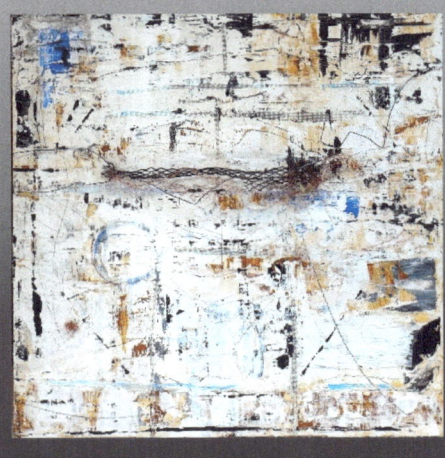
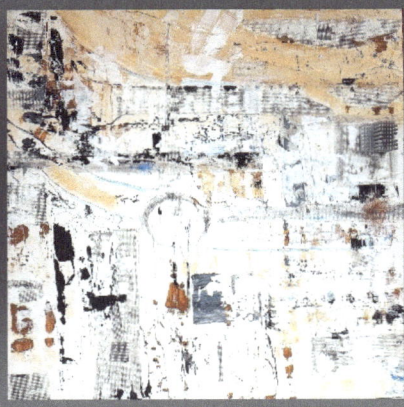
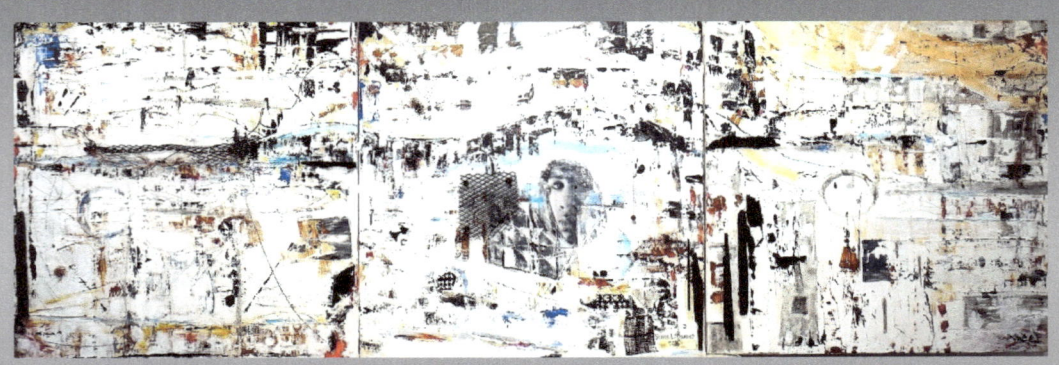

Viewpoints: A Veri'te' (2016) triptych, mixed media on plywood
24"x72"
(details top and full work at bottom)

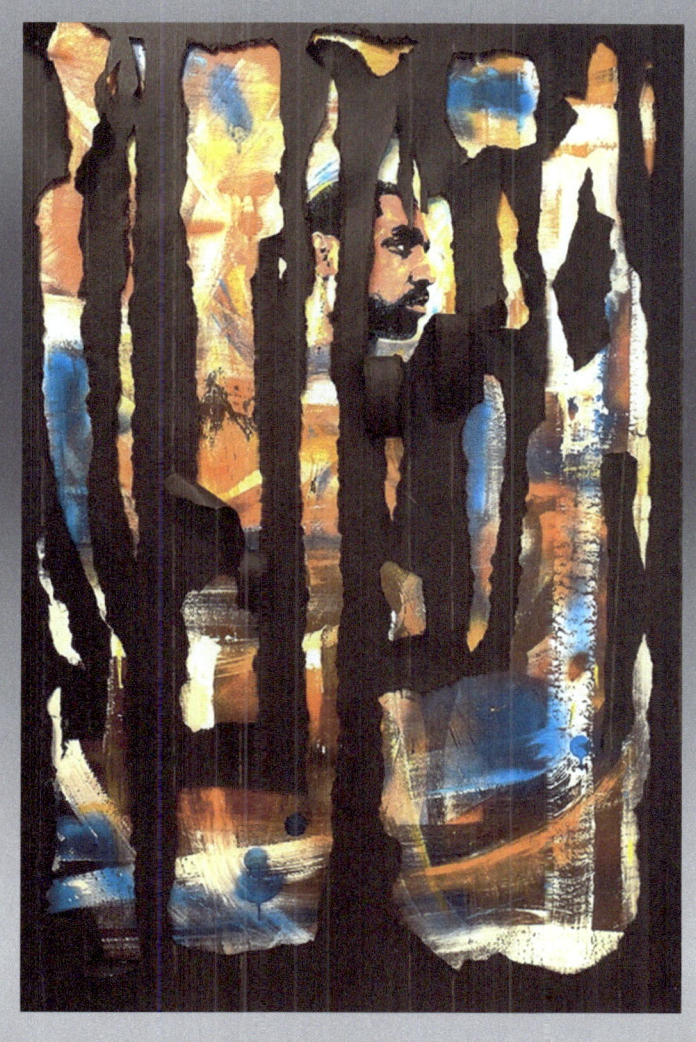

"I am not my skin" (2016)
acrylic, photo transfer, industrial paper on plywood

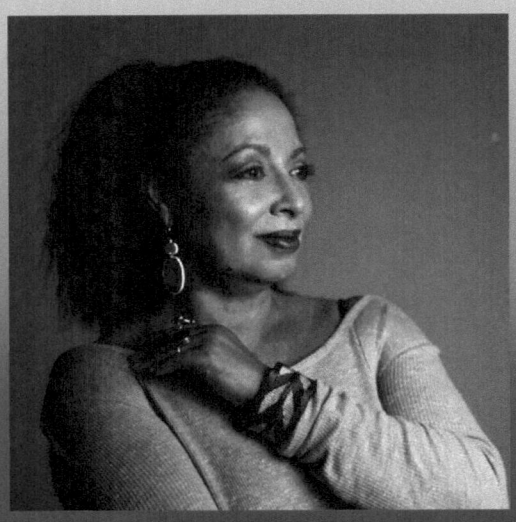

Abbreviated Bio

American artist (African American/Cape Verdean descent). Born in Sacramento, CA; lives and works in Los Angeles.

Ms. Barnes was inspired as a young student by her college professor, artist and art historian, Dr. Samella Lewis. She later studied formal painting, drawing and color theory at Otis College of Art & Design. In addition to her art studies, Ms. Barnes earned a B.A. in Communications that included work in video, film and communications theory, that has contributed to her approach to visually framing an idea and infusing semiotics. Ms. Barnes has exhibited her work in major cities of the U.S. and in the Republic of Panama.

Past Museum Shows

2015   "Hard Edged: Geometrical Abstraction and Beyond", California African American Museum, Los Angeles, curator Mar Hollingsworth

2005   "Pathways": A Survey of African American Artists in Los Angeles 1966-1989, California African American Museum/Los Angeles Municipal Art Gallery, curators Mark Steven Greenfield and Dale Brockman Davis; <u>Two Person Artist Talk:</u> Dr. Samella Lewis and Sharon Louise Barnes

Contact Information:

Website: www.sharonlouisebarnes.com
Email: slbart@att.net
Instagram: @sharonbarnes4702

ISBM-13: 978-197384005

All artwork images ©2017

Sharon Louise Barnes

www.ingramcontent.com/pod-product-compliance
Lightning Source LLC
Chambersburg PA
CBHW041946240526
45473CB00033B/627